DESERT DISCOVERIES

WRITTEN BY
GINGER WADSWORTH

ILLUSTRATED BY
JOHN CARROZZA

iɷi Charlesbridge

Text copyright © 1997 by Ginger Wadsworth
Illustrations copyright © 1997 by John Carrozza
All rights reserved, including the right of
reproduction in whole or in part in any form.

Published by Charlesbridge Publishing
85 Main Street
Watertown, MA 02172-4411
(617) 926-0329

Printed in the United States of America

(hc) 10 9 8 7 6 5 4 3 2 1
(sc) 10 9 8 7 6 5 4 3 2 1

Library of Congress Cataloging-in-Publication Data
Wadsworth, Ginger.
    Desert discoveries/by Ginger Wadsworth; illustrated by John Carrozza.
        p. cm.
Summary: Describes the behavior of thirteen different animals—including jackrabbits,
roadrunners, tarantulas, and rattlesnakes—during a day in the desert.
        ISBN 0-88106-818-7 (reinforced hardcover)
        ISBN 0-88106-817-9 (softcover)
        1. Desert animals—Juvenile literature. 2. Desert ecology—Juvenile literature. [1. Desert
animals. 2. Desert ecology. 3. Ecology.]
I. Carrozza, John, 1958– ill. II. Title.
QL116.W32 1997
591.909'54—dc20   95-24614

The illustrations in this book are done in Luma watercolors on Lanaquarelle watercolor paper.
The display type and text type were set in Tiepolo and Zorba by Diane M. Earley.
Color separations were made by Pure Imaging, Watertown, Massachusetts.
Printed and bound by Worzalla Publishing Company, Stevens Point, Wisconsin
Production supervision by Brian G. Walker
Designed by Diane M. Earley

At first glance, the desert looks big and empty. Much of the time, dry winds blow across the land, where less than ten inches of rain falls each year. Although there are some cold deserts, most are hot, with long days of sun and drought.

But take a second look! The desert is a land of surprises. In the spring, wildflowers often carpet large areas. During the cooler winter season, snow might dust the desert briefly or coat the surrounding mountains and plateaus. Cacti and other plants have learned to survive in the desert. So have many animals, birds, and insects.

Turn the page. It's time to discover some of these desert dwellers.

While the grasses are still damp with dew, black-tailed hares, which are commonly called jackrabbits, nibble flowers, seeds, and grasses. These herbivores have big ears that help them listen for danger and help them stay cool. Jackrabbits give off body heat through these paper-thin ears. Their bulging eyes provide a wide-angle view of the desert. With their long, powerful hind legs, jackrabbits are some of the fastest runners in the desert. When the hot sun is overhead, they rest in the shade. They often lie in the bowl-shaped forms they have made in the sand.

Look for the jackrabbit resting in its
bowl-shaped form under a bush!

Before midmorning a covey of quail darts about beneath a palo verde tree. A mother quail and her baby chicks peck the ground, hunting for seeds and bugs. Sometimes they take dust baths in the sand to rid their feathers of tiny bugs. The father quail sits on a branch, proudly watching his family. He also looks for hungry hawks, coyotes, or snakes. In case of danger, the father quail gives an alarm call, which signals the covey to scatter.

How many quail do you see?

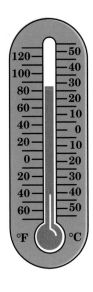

The sun inches higher in the sky and warms the desert. Tortoises soak up the morning sun through their thick shells, or carapaces. When it gets too hot, they often decide to go underground into their burrows. They dig tunnels with their front legs and, like bulldozers, push and shove away the dirt with their hind feet. Never in a hurry, they plod across the sand in search of plants, berries, and flowers to eat. When they need protection from a hungry coyote or a curious raven, they quickly pull their head, legs, and tail inside their shell. Right now scientists are worried about the desert tortoise's future because its natural habitat is slowly being destroyed.

Try to figure out which is a desert tortoise and which are just rocks!

During the heat of the day, most desert animals stay in the shade, but not roadrunners. These ground-loving birds seem to have endless energy. If they get too hot, they pant through their beaks to cool down. And instead of flying, they love to run up and down the sandy washes. They can go from zero to about fifteen miles per hour in a few seconds. Their long tails help them make sharp turns. They eat insects, snakes, and lizards, which they usually swallow head first.

Look for a roadrunner with
a lizard's tail in its beak!

Lizards are reptiles, with dry, scaly skin. They look similar to little dragons. Most of them like to run around on the rocks and sand, or sunbathe. They eat plants, insects, and spiders. Many kinds of lizards live in the desert, and most of them are harmless. This Gila monster is different from many lizards. It usually comes out at dusk or in the afternoon. Gila monsters are covered on top with rounded, beadlike scales and walk with a waddle in search of eggs and insects. They have a poisonous bite.

Can you find a Gila monster?
How many other lizards do you see?

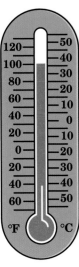

By late afternoon, when the desert begins to cool down, tarantula spiders wake up in their web-lined holes in the ground. Tarantulas are large spiders covered with prickly brown or black hair. They move across the desert on eight legs in search of food. Most of the time, tarantulas seem to walk in slow motion: one leg up, one leg down. But when they see insects or smaller spiders to eat, they act quickly. Tarantulas stab their fangs into their victims and kill them with venom. These spiders seldom attack people, but if they do, the bite is similar to a bee sting.

Try to find the tarantula!

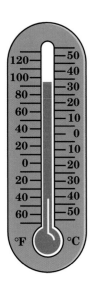

For a while, a multicolored sunset fills the sky before darkness sets in. It is time for the bats to wake up and hunt for food. Thousands of bats spin, dive, dip, and swoop across the sky while making high-pitched sounds in their throats. These sounds, as many as fifty thousand per second, bounce off objects of all sizes and travel back to the bats' ears. This echolocation helps them find food in the dark. All night long, some species of bats scoop up flying insects and eat them. Other species dine on fruit, nectar, and pollen. During the day, bats hang upside down in caves or other dark places to sleep.

How many bats do
you see in the sky?

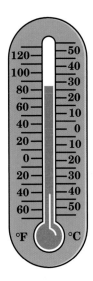

Most snakes come out in the evening when the air and land are warm, not hot. That's because they are cold-blooded. Their body temperature constantly adjusts to the air and the land surrounding them. Snakes are covered with scales that come in different colors, sizes, and patterns. These scales help them move across the desert. Snakes also use their strong muscles to push and pull themselves along. Many kinds of snakes live in the desert. All snakes are carnivores and swallow their prey whole. Most, including poisonous rattlesnakes, are shy and stay away from people.

How many rattles does the rattlesnake
have at the end of its tail?

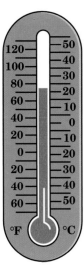

The moon inches above the mountains, casting a pale light on the sand. Kangaroo rats hop around on their long back legs, holding their short front legs under their chins. Their tails help them balance when they jump. At night they gather seeds and stuff them in their fur-lined cheek pouches. These warm-blooded mammals take their food to storage rooms in their underground burrow system of tunnels and rooms. Instead of drinking water from little pools or streams, kangaroo rats make the water they need in their bodies from the food they eat.

Do you see the kangaroo rat
leaping into the air?

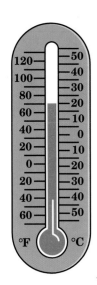

It is midnight, and the moon is high in the sky. During the day, scorpions live under dilapidated buildings, dried cacti limbs, or rocks and at night they come out to eat. Scorpions have eight legs and grow to be one to five inches long. They capture spiders, insects, and smaller scorpions in their crablike pinchers. Then they stab their prey with the stinger on the tip of their tail, poisoning the victim with their venom. Only one or two species are poisonous enough to harm a person. Just to be safe, don't touch one!

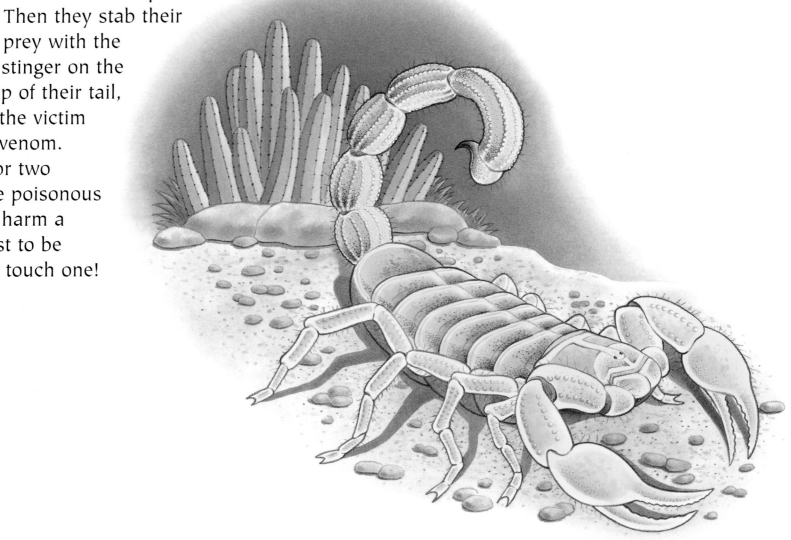

Do you see the scorpion?

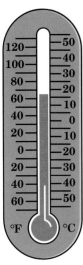

During the heat of day, coyotes nap under plants or sleep in their dens. In the late afternoon and night, they prowl the desert looking for food. They will eat or hunt anything: vegetables, fruit, carrion, or small animals such as rabbits and mice. Sometimes they travel in groups, or bands. Coyotes look like lean dogs with bushy tails and big ears. They love to bark, yip, and yowl during the night.

Try to find the coyote singing
in the moonlight.

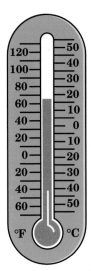

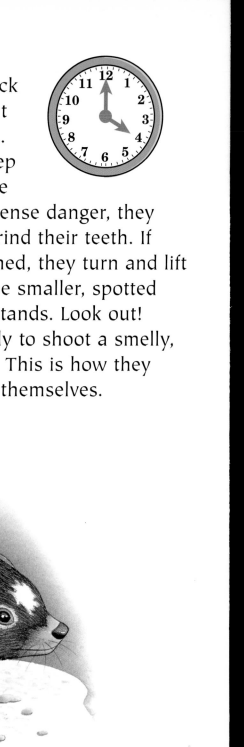

Most nights in the desert, millions of stars decorate the ink-black sky. The striped and spotted skunks are nocturnal and come out at night to eat and to play with other skunks. During the day, these mammals sleep in tunnels that they dig under the rocks. When striped skunks sense danger, they stamp their front feet or grind their teeth. If they really feel threatened, they turn and lift their bushy tails. The smaller, spotted skunks do handstands. Look out! They are ready to shoot a smelly, oily spray. This is how they defend themselves.

Count the baby spotted skunks
following their mother.

As the sun rises, desert bighorn sheep graze on grass, plants, twigs, and cactus fruit. Males, called rams, have large curved horns; females, called ewes, have shorter horns. Their habitat is usually rocky places where there are few people. They use their sharp eyesight to spot predators, like mountain lions, bobcats, or human hunters. In case of danger, the surefooted bighorn sheep escape through steep canyons and cliffs to mountaintops.

How many bighorn sheep do you see?

Now you have discovered thirteen different creatures who live in the desert.

Try to see how many of them you can name!

Glossary

There are about twenty major desert biomes in the world on five continents. Deserts cover about one-seventh of the earth's land surface. *Desert Discoveries* was influenced by the author's interest in the deserts of the southwestern United States and Mexico.

band: a group of animals.

biome: scientists have divided the world into units, or parts, that have similar plants, animals, and climates. The desert is a land biome.

burrow: a hole or tunnel in the ground made by an animal.

cactus: a fleshy desert plant, usually leafless and spiny, that often produces beautiful spring flowers.

carapace: a hard shell covering the back of an animal.

carnivore: a flesh-eating animal.

carrion: a dead animal.

cold-blooded: having a body temperature the same as the land and air.

covey: a small flock, or group, of similar birds.

den: a cave, hole, or hollow space that an animal uses as a shelter, home, and place to bear young.

echolocation: a system by which an animal sends out beeps or pulses of high-pitched sounds and listens for the echoes that bounce back when the sounds hit an object.

ewe: an adult female sheep.

fangs: long, sharp, hollow or grooved teeth through which poison is injected.

form: a shallow, scooped-out area in the soil where an animal rests during the heat of the day.

graze: to feed on grass or plants.

habitat: the area in which a plant or animal species lives naturally.

hare: closely related to rabbits, hares have longer hind legs and ears and usually live alone.

herbivore: a plant-eating animal.

horn: a hard growth made of a hairlike material that forms around bony cores on the heads of many hoofed mammals. Unlike antlers, horns are permanent.

mammals: any group of warm-blooded animals with backbones, including human beings, that feeds its young with milk from the female milk glands.

nectar: a sweet-tasting liquid released by plants.

nocturnal: active at night.

palo verde tree: a desert tree with a green trunk and branches and yellow flowers. *Palo verde* means "green twig" in Spanish.

pollen: the powdery, yellow grains that are the male reproductive cells of flowering plants.

predator: an animal, bird, or insect that hunts and captures another creature for food.

prey: an animal, insect, or bird that is hunted for food.

ram: a mature male sheep.

reptiles: snakes, lizards, and turtles; air-breathing, cold-blooded vertebrates, usually covered with scales.

scales: small, thin protective plates that cover the bodies of lizards and snakes.

species: a group of related plants or animals that can mate and produce young like themselves.

venom: the poisonous fluid released by certain snakes, spiders, and scorpions, usually by biting or stinging their prey.

warm-blooded: mammals and birds with a blood temperature that remains the same, no matter what the temperature of the land, air, or water.

wash: a small, sandy streambed with low banks.

web: the thin, silken material spun by spiders and some insects.